JUST AS YOU ARE

Celebrating the Wonder of Unconditional Love

Written by
Jen Harrison

Illustrated by
Michelle Catanach

"Just as you are",
Love,
Jen xo

First published in 2019
by Inside Out Publishing

www.insideoutpublishing.com

Text and illustrations copyright © 2019 Jen Harrison.

A catalogue record for this book is available from the
British Library.

ISBN: 978-1-9162504-2-0

For all the children of the world.

"You are lovable my dear, more than you know. You are
amazing, wonderful and kind. You are loved right now
from your head to your toes

JUST AS YOU ARE."

"Let me tell you a story," Mommy said, "about who
you really are.
The truth is the truth,
And it will never change or go very far.

"You are lovable my dear,

More than you know.

You are amazing, wonderful and kind.

You are loved right now from your head to your toes

JUST

AS

YOU

ARE.

"There's nothing you need to do,
To earn my love.
It came with you when you were born,
It was sent from up above.

"You'll *always* be enough,
You'll always be sweet.
You were born that way, my love,
From your head right down to your feet.

"Believe that the words I say are true.
You can reach for the stars –
There's not a thing you cannot do.

Your love is eternal,
It was given to you before birth,
So there's not a thing that you need to do
To find it here on Earth."

Little bear rubbed his eyes. He thought that he needed to be good at *everything*, to be loved.

"What about when I get my homework wrong,
And I can't remember the words to a song?

"When I climb a step and then I fall
And I just don't believe that I can do it at all?"

Mommy bear scooped little bear up in her arms.

"Yes, you are right," said Mommy, "those things may
happen –
We are *all* going to make mistakes.
But one thing remains true through all of that,
And that truth can never be replaced.

"You are lovable my dear,

More than you know.

You are amazing, wonderful and kind.

You are loved right now from your head to your toes

JUST AS YOU ARE

"There is nothing you need to do,
To earn my love.
It came with you when you were born,
It was sent from up above.

"You'll *always* be enough,
You'll always be sweet.
You were born that way, my love,
From your head right down to your feet.

"Believe that the words I say are true.
You can reach for the stars –
There's not a thing you cannot do.

"Your love is eternal,
It was given to you before birth.
So there's not a thing that you need to do
To find it here on Earth."

Little bear began to feel warm inside.

"I really am lovable
So I don't need to fear.
And when I forget that I'm loved
I can just remember that you're
near..."

But he *still* had questions ...

"What about when my friends don't want to play

Or they tell me to go away?

What about when I'm tired

And I don't feel understood?

Or when I'm upset and angry

And don't behave as well as I could?"

"Yes you're right, my dear," said Mommy.
"Sometimes you *do* feel angry or tired,
And your friends may not want to play.
But that doesn't change a single thing,
About how lovable you are today.

"You are lovable my dear,

More than you know.

You are amazing, wonderful and kind.

You are loved right now from your head to your toes

JUST AS YOU ARE.

"There is nothing you need to do,
To earn my love.
It came with you when you were born,
It was sent from up above.

"You'll *always* be enough,
You'll always be sweet.
You were born that way, my love,
From your head right down to your feet.

"Believe that the words I say are true.
You can reach for the stars –
There's not a thing you cannot do.

"Your love is eternal,
It was given to you before birth.
So there's not a thing that you need to do
To find it here on Earth."

Little bear began to feel that he was
lovable, just as he is.

"So I really am great,
And it's okay to make mistakes.
Because I'm loved to my bones,
And that will never change..."

But he *still* had questions ...

"How about when my friend runs faster than me,
Or I think I need to be more like my brother?
I sometimes feel like I'm missing something,
And that I'm not as good as another."

"Yes little one, that's right," said Mommy.

"Others *may* run faster than you.

But you're not missing a thing

And how loved you are will never change,

Because one thing *always* remains true.

"You are lovable my dear,

More than you know.

You are amazing, wonderful and kind.

You are loved right now from your head to your toes

JUST AS YOU ARE.

"There's nothing you need
to do,
To earn my love.
It came with you when you
were born,
It was sent from up above.

"You'll *always* be enough,
You'll always be sweet.
You were born that way, my love,
From your head right down to your feet.

"Believe that the words I say are true.
You can reach for the stars –
There's not a thing you cannot do.

"Your love is eternal,
It was given to you before birth,
So there's not a thing that you need to do
To find it here on Earth."

Little bear felt loved.

But he *still* had questions ...

"Well how about when I kicked a ball,
And it hit my friend on the head?

"Or when it's getting late and it's past my bedtime
And I'm not yet asleep in my bed?"

"Yes my dear," said Mommy, "you made mistakes,
You did things that didn't feel good.
And through all those mistakes and things that you did,
You are lovable and loved."

Little bear's smile grew bigger and bigger.

"I'm just loved as I am?
Nothing that I need to do, no need to try?
I'm loved from my head to my toes
And I don't need to ask why?

"Wow this is real!
I can feel this, I really can!
I am me, I am loved
And I am lovable

JUST
AS
I
AM."

Mommy bear put her nose on
little bear's nose.

"Yes my dear, all of that is true.
From your head to your toes,
This is real, this is you.
And there is someone who knows ...

"Who you are,

And how you shine.

All of that love is here for you,

There really isn't a thing that you need to do."

And with a big happy sigh,
Both bears fell asleep,
Feeling snuggly and warm,
As they lay there cheek to cheek.

Both having sweet dreams,
Knowing that they were loved from afar,
Feeling happy and lovable

JUST AS THEY ARE.

My Thoughts and Feelings

1. Why do you think the young bear thought that he wasn't as good as other bears?

2. Why do you think he worries that he has to get his homework right and he's worried about making a mistake?

3. Can you think of a time when you thought that you needed to be like your friends or thought that you weren't good at something? What did you learn from Mother bear about this?

4. What do you think it means to be loved and lovable?

5. How do you feel when you feel lovable?

6. How do you feel when you worry about making a mistake? Where do you feel that worry in your body?

Can you spot these on the pages...?

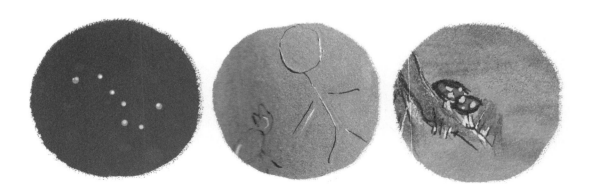

About the Author
Jen Harrison

Jen Harrison is an advocate for children's mental health and emotional wellbeing and is a consultant working with parents to build their child's self-esteem.

It is clear to Jen that self-esteem begins at home and in the early years, and that the message of unconditional love is essential in order for children to know their self worth and be happy.

One thing that Jen knows to be true is that we cannot teach growth mindset or build a child's self-confidence without first laying the firm foundation within a child that they are lovable no matter what. It is only when a child knows who they really are and what their self-worth is, that they can flourish in their learning and growth. Unconditional love REALLY is the number one thing that we all need before anything else. Children then feel free to make mistakes as they learn and grow and no longer try to strive for perfection in the hopes that they will earn their self-worth. They come to learn through messages like those in this story, that they already have self-worth deep inside of them and it was there all along.

Having said that, Jen also understands that it's never too late to learn about the truth of who you really are and invites both adults and children alike to enjoy and embrace this heart-filled message.

 www.sensitivechild.co.uk

 /the_sensitive_adult_and_child

 /thesensitiveadultandchild

Acknowledgements

A big thank you goes out to the illustrator Michelle Catanach for taking my words and this story and bringing it to life... I know so many children (and adults!) are going to love these illustrations! It's been a joy working on this book with you.

Thank you to those special friends and family in my life who have shown me what unconditional love looks and feels like... you've blessed my life in more ways than I can describe.

And I can't forget to thank my school teacher when I was aged five who said I would one day write a book and all the people who have come into my life since that day who have inspired me to do it.

All of this was possible because of God and His great love. I'm grateful to have been involved in the process of such a wonderful message that wanted to be written. And what a message that is needed. Thank you.

Lightning Source UK Ltd.
Milton Keynes UK
UKHW051318160120
357042UK00004B/67/P